Bossa Nova & Samba
FOR Guitar

---

by Mike Christiansen

ONLINE AUDIO

To Access the Online Audio Go To:
www.melbay.com/20608MEB

Online Audio

INTRODUCTION

With their origins in Brazil, *bossa nova* (*new music*) and samba (from *semba* meaning belly-dance) with their syncopated rhythms, rich harmonies, and haunting melodies have become popular music styles the world over. From recordings to the concert stage to restaurants and clubs, these styles of music have been warmly embraced by audiences of all ages. The guitar plays an essential role in bossa nova and samba. Its mellow, percussive quality, and ability to display rich sophisticated harmonies, make it the perfect accompaniment and solo instrument for these styles. This book presents many of the components used in playing bossa nova and samba music on the guitar. The majority of the contents will focus on accompaniment styles and techniques. There are also sections explaining theoretical concepts pertaining to harmony and rhythm and sections presenting chords commonly used in bossa nova and samba.

As well as listening to the accompanying CD, it is recommended that the student listen to various artists who are masters of the bossa nova and samba such as: Antonio Carlos Jobim, Edu Lobo, Eumir Deodato, Leila Pinheira, João Gilberto, Luis Bonfa, João Bosco, and Caetano Veloso.

A special thanks to Antonio Adolfo, Thiago Trajano, and Ary Dias whose instruction was invaluable.

NOTATION

Before showing some of the common fingerings of chords often used in playing bossa nova, there needs to be some explanation of the type of notation that will be used throughout this book when presenting accompaniment patterns and techniques. The following shows the identification symbols used for left and right hands:

Left Hand
1 = index finger
2 = middle finger
3 = ring finger
4 = little finger

Right Hand
P = thumb (pulgar *)
i = index finger (indice *)
m = middle finger (media *)
a = ring finger (angular *)

For the accompaniment notation used in this book, the letter P will indicate the picking of a single bass string with the right-hand thumb. The letter P is often used to identify the right-hand thumb. The bass note, played with the right-hand thumb, will often be the lowest note of the chord and usually be on strings six or five. The lowest note of the chord will often be the root. The note has the same letter name as the chord. The P may have a stem under it (P or P) indicating the time value of the stroke. A strum bar (/) gets the time value of a quarter note. A stem under the P indicates the thumb stroke gets the time value of a quarter note. A strum bar or a P with a stem and a flag (/ P) have the time value of an eighth note. A dot behind a strum bar or a P (/· P·) lengthens the finger-stroke or the thumb-stroke by half its original value.

A strum bar (/) indicates that strings two, three and four are played simultaneously with the right-hand fingers a, m, and i. An upstroke and a free stroke should be used and all the strings should be allowed to ring. Throughout this book, this will be referred to as a *finger-stroke*. Strings one, two, and three or strings two, three, and four may be played. The grouping used will depend on the chord or the desired sound. Generally, the grouping of strings two, three, and four is more common and gives a more mellow sound.

The following example shows how the playing of a C6/9 chord, with the bass alternating with a finger-stroke, would be notated. The standard notation is written on the right, and the notation used in this book is written on the left. In the example on the left, the stem under the P indicates the time value of a quarter note. The strum bar (/) also has the time value of a quarter note. Generally, unless indicated by a rest or a staccato mark when the finger-stroke precedes a thumb stroke, the chord should be allowed to ring though the thumb stroke. The thumb-stroke should also ring through a following finger-stroke. This is illustrated below:

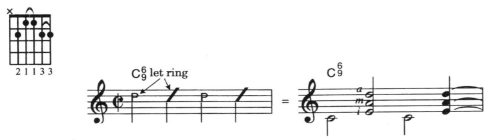

* in spanish language

3

If a thumb-stroke or finger-stroke has a dot above it (⸍ ṗ), play staccato. This means the sound should be short. This can be accomplished by releasing the left-hand pressure on the strings quickly after stroking them. Be careful not to lift the left-hand fingers completely off the strings... just release the pressure making the sound short.

If the letter P is written under a strum bar (⸍ P), the right-hand thumb is played at the same time as the right-hand fingers.

The examples in this book will be written in cut time (₵). This is because **it is crucial that when playing bossa nova, the music has to have a strong 2 feel** (two beats in a measure). Many lead sheets and sheet music will show bossa novas written in $\frac{4}{4}$, when actually, the more Brazilian way of writing the music would be in $\frac{2}{4}$. To achieve the two-beat feel, cut time will be used.

FOUR-STRING CHORDS

Because of the rich harmonies and embellishments used in Brazilian music, four-string chords are commonly used. Some of the more common four-string chords are presented in this section of the book. Four-string chords are also referred to as dead-string chords because some of the strings in the chord are intentionally muted or deadened. Muted strings are indicated with an "X" written above the string on the chord diagram. To mute a string, tilt a left-hand finger and lightly touch the string(s) to be muted. Four-string chords are often selected over barre chords for the sake of fingering, and many chords (i.e. 6, maj7, etc.) sound better when played with four-string chords. Another rationale for using the four-string chords is that none of the notes are doubled as they are in barre chords. This lack of doubling gives the chord a less cluttered sound.

Each four-string chord from the first category has the root (note with the same letter name as the chord) on the sixth string. Each four-string chord from the second category has the root on the fifth string. The charts for locating the roots on the sixth and fifth strings are shown above each category. For the chord to have the correct letter name, the root (on the sixth string for the first category) should be placed in the fret number corresponding to the letter name of the chord. For example, Gmaj7 from the first category is played with the finger on the sixth string in the third fret because G is found in the third fret.

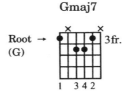

Muting the strings, indicated with the x, is important if these chords are strummed. However, in the bossa nova styles, rather than strumming these chords, the bass (lowest note in the chord) is played with the thumb and strings 2, 3, and 4 (or occasionally 1, 2, and 3) are played with the right hand fingers a, m and i.

Location of Sixth-String Root

Fret →	0	1	3	5	7	8	10	12
Root Name →	E	F	G	A	B	C	D	E

FIRST CATEGORY
(Sixth-String Root)

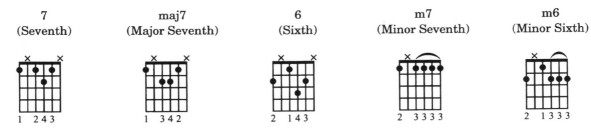

5

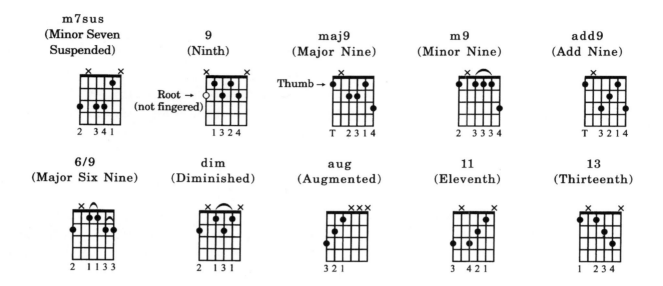

Practice the following progressions which contain four-string chords from the first category. For now, play the chord exercises by either alternating the thumb with the fingers (as shown in the first example below), or play the thumb with the fingers (as shown in the second example below). The thumb should play the sixth string (the lowest note of the chord).

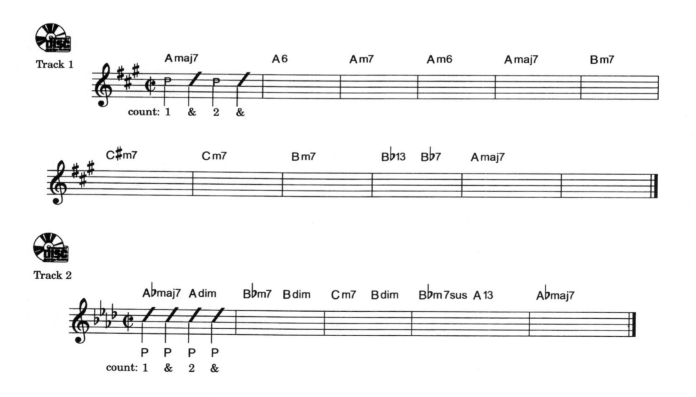

6

Location of Fifth-String Roots

Fret →	0	2	3	5	7	8	10	12
Root Name →	A	B	C	D	E	F	G	A

SECOND CATEGORY
(Fifth-String Roots)

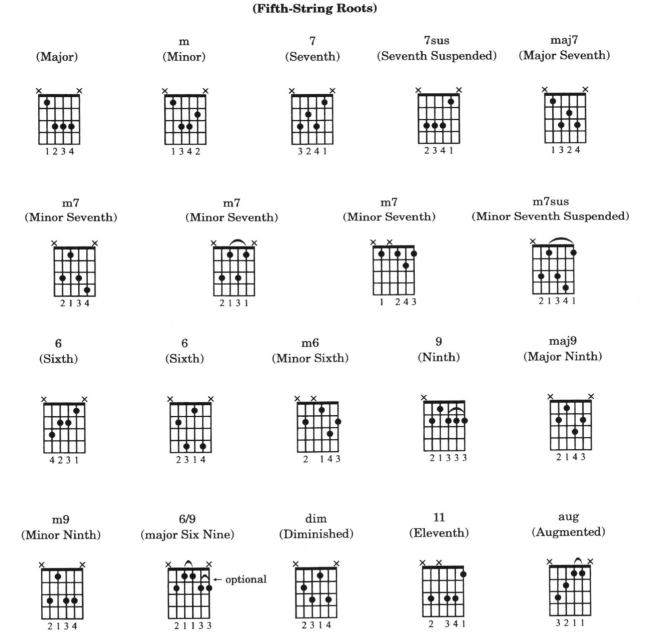

The following progressions should be practiced using four-string chords from the second category. Play the fifth string with the thumb.

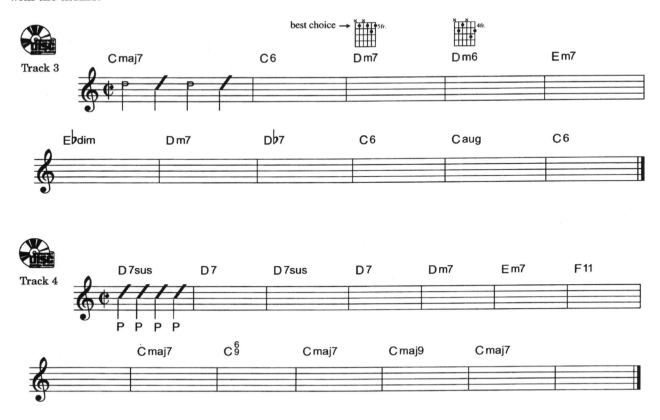

Knowing both categories of four-string chords will keep the chord changes closer together. Practice the following progressions using both categories of four-string chords. The R/6 and the R/5 above the chord names indicate whether the root of the chord is on the sixth or fifth sting. The R/6 and R/5 will help in determining which category of four-string chord to use. Remember, pick the lowest note of the chord with the right-hand thumb.

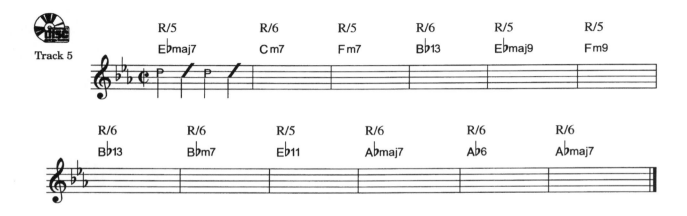

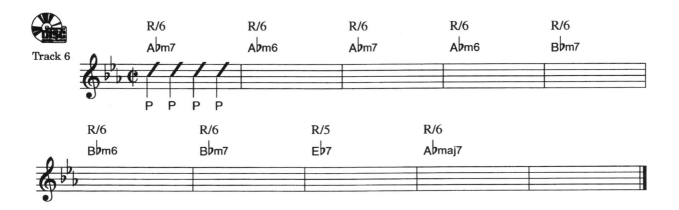

Use the most convenient four-string chords to play the following progression. Use both categories of four-string chords and keep the chords close together.

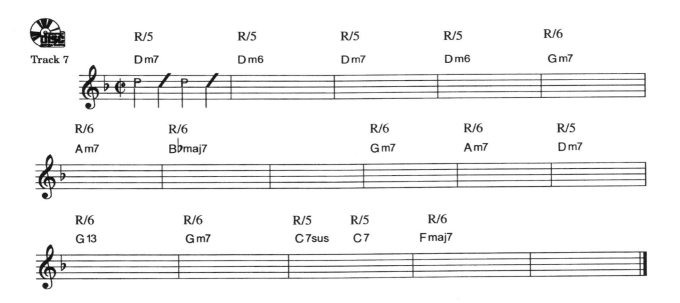

ALTERED CHORDS

In an altered chord, certain intervals (the fifth, ninth, and eleventh) may be sharp or flat. Altered chords are used to add color and a strong sense of "pull" leading into the next chord. Altered chords add color to the music. The following diagrams show fingerings for many of the commonly used altered chords. The "R" shows the locations of the root in the chord.

7♭5
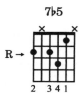

7♭5

7♭5

7♭5

7+
(or 7+5, or +7)
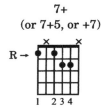

♯5
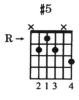

7♭9
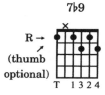

7♭9

7♯9

7♯9

7♭5♯9

7♯5♭9

7♯5♭9   7♯5♯9   7♯5♯9
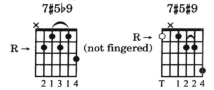

7♯5♯9

7♭5♭9
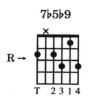

7♭5♭9
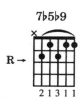

maj7♯11
(or maj7♭5)
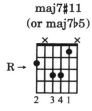

maj7♯11
(or maj7♭5)
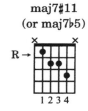

m7♭5
(also called half
diminished or ø)
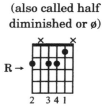

m7♭5

maj9♯11
(or maj9♭5)
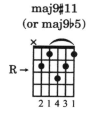

6/9♯11
(or 6/9♭5)
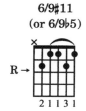

6/9♯11   13♭9
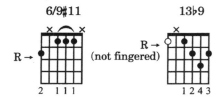

10

Practice the following progression containing altered chords. For now, use the [P / P /] pattern, or the [/ / / /] pattern to play each measure. Be sure to pick the lowest note of the chord with the right-hand thumb.

Track 8

| Dm7 | G7(#5) | Cmaj7 | | Dm7 | G7+ (same as 7(#5)) | Cmaj7 |

| Bm7(♭5) | B♭7(♭5) | Am7 | | Dm7 | G7(#5♭9) |

| Cmaj7 | | Em7(♭5) | A7 | Dm7 | G7(♭9) | Cmaj7 |

| Em7 | A7 | Am7 | D7(♭9) | Gmaj7 | |

| D7(#9) | Gmaj7 | D7(#9) | Gmaj7 | Am7 | D7(♭5♭9) | G$\frac{6}{9}$ |

| Am7 | D7(♭5#9) | G$\frac{6}{9}$ | | Am7 | D9 |

| Gmaj7(#11) | Gmaj7 | Dm7 | G7(♭5) | C$\frac{6}{9}$(#11) | C$\frac{6}{9}$ |

SYNCOPATION

Syncopation is one of the most integral elements of bossa nova. Syncopation means accenting in an unexpected place. When many of the notes are played on the second half of the beat (the up beat), the music is syncopated. Rather than having two eighth notes be tied, it is more common and "note efficient" to let one quarter note take the place of two eighth notes. Syncopation, with the quarter note getting one beat, is shown below:

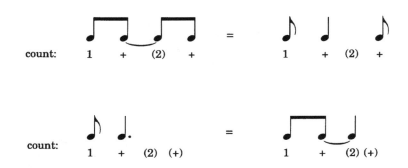

When writing syncopation in $\frac{4}{4}$, the quarter can be placed between beats one and two or between beats three and four. If syncopation occurs between beats two and three, the eighth notes are tied.

Syncopated rhythms are one of the identifying marks of playing bossa nova rhythm guitar. Another mark of bossa nova is the strong "two feel" meaning it should feel as if there are two beats in each measure. Much of the music in Brazil is written in $\frac{2}{4}$. However, many of the lead sheets and much of the bossa nova sheet music printed in the United States is written in $\frac{4}{4}$ time. Although it is written in $\frac{4}{4}$, it should still have a strong two-beat feel. To convey this, the examples and accompaniment patterns in this book have been written in cut time, (¢, $\frac{2}{2}$).

Syncopations for cut time and how they are counted are shown below using strum bar and thumb strokes.

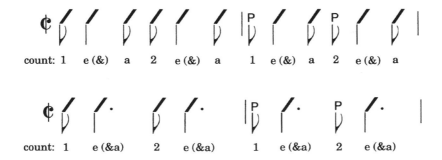

count: 1   e (&)   a   2   e (&)   a   1   e (&)   a   2   e (&)   a

count: 1   e (&a)   2   e (&a)   1   e (&a)   2   e (&a)

Even though in Latin music the beats are subdivided evenly, the accent, the frequent use of syncopation, and the anticipation of beats is sometimes referred to as "Brazilian swing." A typical bossa nova accompaniment pattern used to play one measure of Gmaj7 is shown below.

Gmaj7

pick the sixth string →

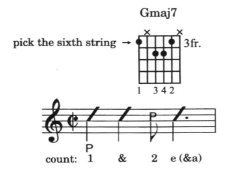

count: 1   &   2   e (&a)

Remember, ⌐ indicates to pick the lowest note of the chord. This will usually be the root, or the note with the same letter name as the chord. ⌐ indicates to play strings 2, 3, and 4 (or 1,2, and 3 depending on the chord and the desired effect) with the right-hand a, m, and i fingers. When a P is written under a strum bar, the thumb is played with the fingers.

ACCOMPANIMENT PATTERNS

It is a misconception that a samba is a bossa nova played at a faster tempo. Actually, there are slow sambas and fast bossa novas. The difference lies in the accent rather than the tempo. In the 1950's, the upper-class people of Brazil wanted a music that was like the samba but did not have the heavy accent and harshness that was played in the samba. The bossa nova was given birth as a result of taking the samba and playing it lighter without the heavy accents. Although the patterns presented in this section of the book are commonly used in bossa nova, they can also be used to play sambas. Later in this book, some other patterns will be presented that can also be used to play sambas. Samba patterns are usually played a bit brighter and with a heavier accent on beat two and the syncopations.

The patterns presented on the next several pages can be used to accompany bossa nova music. The patterns take one measure in ¢ to complete. In as much as many bossa novas and sambas published will appear in $\frac{4}{4}$, these patterns may also be used to play one measure in $\frac{4}{4}$ and can be applied to sheet music and/or lead sheets from fake books. It is important that even if the music is written in $\frac{4}{4}$, that it needs to retain an strong "two feel," rather than feeling like there are four beats to the measure. It needs to be emphasized that **after practicing all of the examples in this book using the one-and two-measure patterns, they can, and should, be applied to playing bossa novas and sambas from music books, sheet music, and lead sheets.**

In bossa nova, often the thumb plays twice in each measure (on beats one and two in cut time). The right-hand thumb can play the root both times in the measure, or the thumb can be used to play the root on the first beat of the measure and then play the fifth of the chord (the note name which is five steps up the major scale from the root) on beat two in cut time. The next example shows how this can be done. In the first measure, the C6/9 is played with the root played twice in the measure. In the second measure, the example shows the root played on the first beat and the fifth of the chord (G) is played in the middle of the measure (on beat two). Whether the root is repeated, or the root and fifth are used, is up to the discretion of the player.

The fifth of the chord should be played below the root rather than above it. In fact, **if the fingering of the chord does not allow the fifth of the chord to be played below the root** (such as a Gmaj7 in the third fret), **play the root on beats one and two rather than alternating the root with the fifth.** Generally, the fifth cannot be played below the root on chords that have the root on the sixth string (such as Gmaj7 in the third fret). Most chords which have the root on the fifth string can have the fifth played below the root. Practice all of the accompaniment patterns in this section of the book playing the root twice in a measure with the right-hand thumb. Then, practice alternating the root with the fifth, providing the fifth may be played below the root.

To achieve a smooth, light feel, let the bass and the chords ring. Avoid heavy accents. The following example is a common two-measure bossa nova accompaniment pattern. Standard notation is written on top, and the notation used in this book is written on the bottom. Remember, when a strum bar is written on top of a P, the right-hand thumb and fingers play together.

Track 9

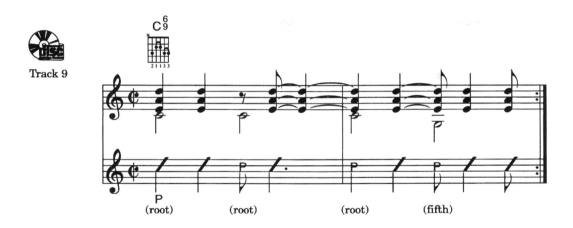

(root)   (root)   (root)   (fifth)

It is extremely important that when a pattern is played which ends on the "a" of beat two, that the chord which is played at the beginning of the next measure be anticipated and played on the "a" of the preceding measure. The frequent use of syncopation and the anticipation of chord changes creates a feeling which is sometimes referred to as Brazilian swing. Even though this term is sometimes used, do not confuse Brazilian swing with the American interpretation of the term swing. In bossa nova and samba (as in all Latin music) the beats are subdivided evenly.

The following example shows how chord changes are anticipaited:

Track 10

Practice each of the patterns in this section of the book holding any single chord and repeat the pattern until it feels comfortable. After practicing a single pattern with one chord, practice playing the patterns and play random chords in each measure. For now, do not play more than one chord per measure. Remember, each pattern takes one measure in ¢ (or $\frac{4}{4}$) to complete, and the patterns should be applied to songbooks, leadsheets, and sheet music. Practice each pattern with the thumb playing the root of the chord on beats one and two. Then, practice each pattern with the thumb playing the root on beat one and the fifth on beat two. Keep the fifth below the root. If that is not possible, play the root on beats one and two. Pattern 1 is the basic pattern. Most of the other patterns are variations on pattern 1.

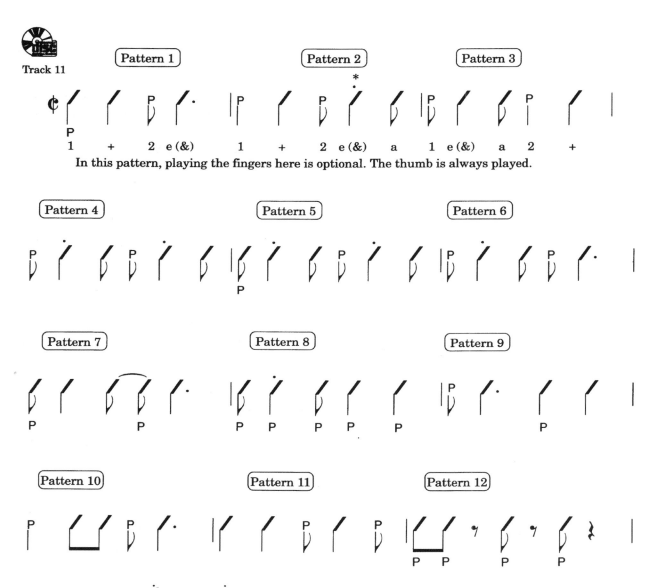

In this pattern, playing the fingers here is optional. The thumb is always played.

* The staccato strum (⸓) or pick (P⸳) is done by quickly releasing the left-hand fingers after stroking the strings, so the sound is short. Lift the finger up, but not off of the strings. The staccato is optional.

Play the following examples using the rhythm written in the first measure to play all of the measures in the pieces. After playing the exercises as written, select one of the other accompaniment patterns to play each exercise.

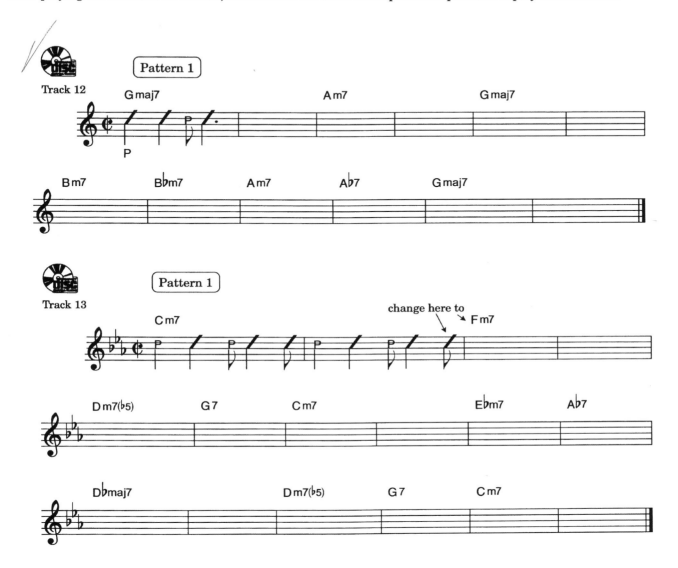

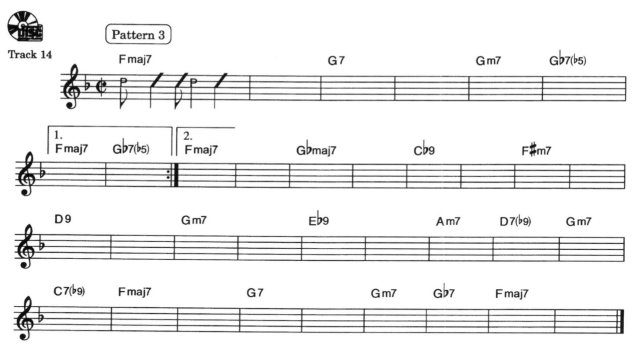

The same accompaniment pattern does not have to be used to play each measure. Various combinations of the patterns can be used in the same piece of music. The next example shows how this would be done. The shifting from pattern to pattern can occur randomly. Practice the next example changing from pattern 1 to pattern 2 and pattern 8 in different locations.

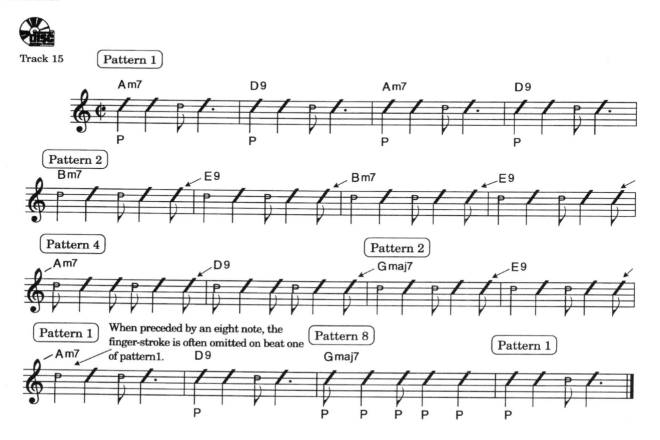

The next example shows how several of the other patterns can be combined. Written in parentheses above each measure is the number of the pattern being used in that measure.

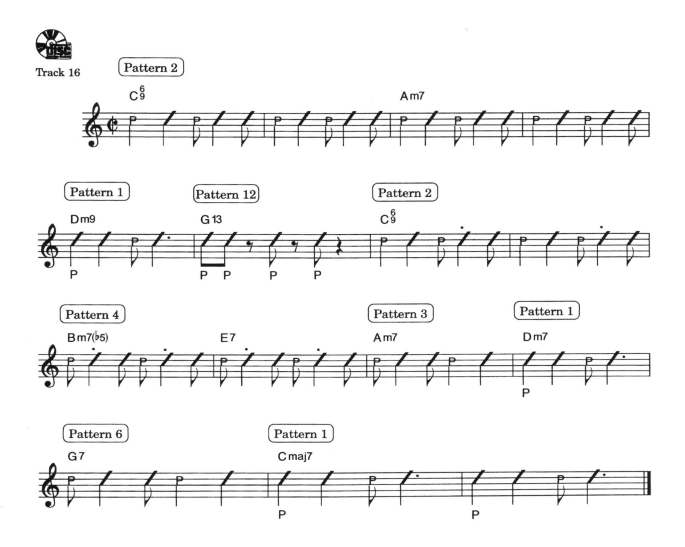

TWO-MEASURE PATTERNS

The following patterns can be used to accompany bossa nova. Each pattern takes two measures in cut time to complete. The patterns may also be applied to two measures in $\frac{4}{4}$. The techniques involved in converting these two-measure patterns from bossa nova to more of a samba feel will be presented later in this book. As with the one-measure patterns, if a two-measure pattern is being played which ends on the "a" of beat two (in cut time), and the chord changes after the two-measure pattern, the new chord will anticipate beat one and be played on the "a" of the previous measure. The following example shows how this is done:

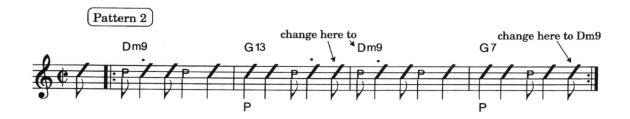

Practice each two-measure pattern holding one chord, and then randomly change chords while playing the patterns. After doing that, practice the exercises that follow the patterns. Each pattern takes two measures in ¢ to complete. These patterns can also be applied to music written in $\frac{4}{4}$. In that case, each pattern takes two measures in $\frac{4}{4}$ to complete. When you feel comfortable playing the exercises, use these patterns to play bossa novas and sambas from sheet music and lead sheets.

Track 17

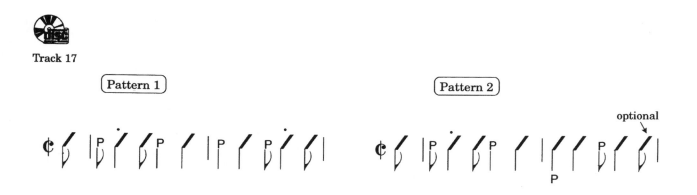

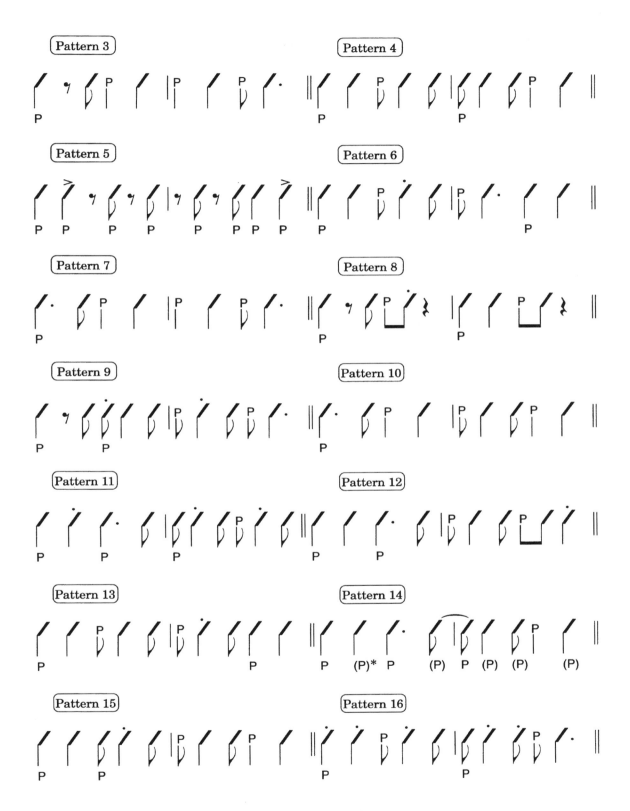

* The P in parentheses indicates that the thumb stroke is optional.

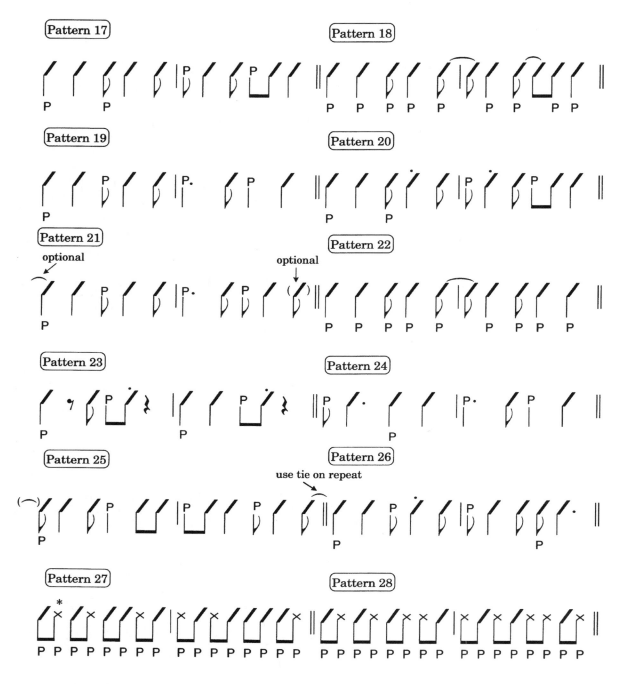

* In patterns 27 and 28, whenever the right-hand fingers play, the thumb plays also. The patterns imitate the sound of the tamborim which is one of the percussion instruments used in bossa nova and samba. The pattern can be played with or without heavy accents. The strum bars with an X on them (⤬) indicate a muted sound. This effect is achieved by lifting the left-hand fingers slightly (not off of the strings) and playing the strings with the right-hand fingers and thumb. This will create a muted or dampened sound. The thumb stroke is also muted.

Play the following exercises using the two-measure accompaniment patterns.

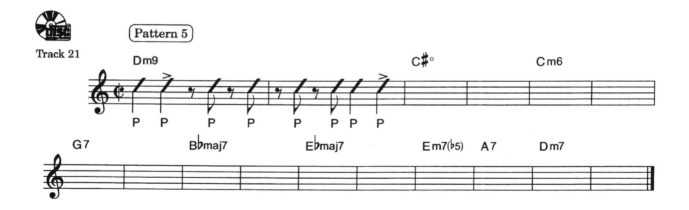

One and two-measure patterns can be combined in the same piece. The next two examples show how this can be done. The brackets indicate the length of each pattern.

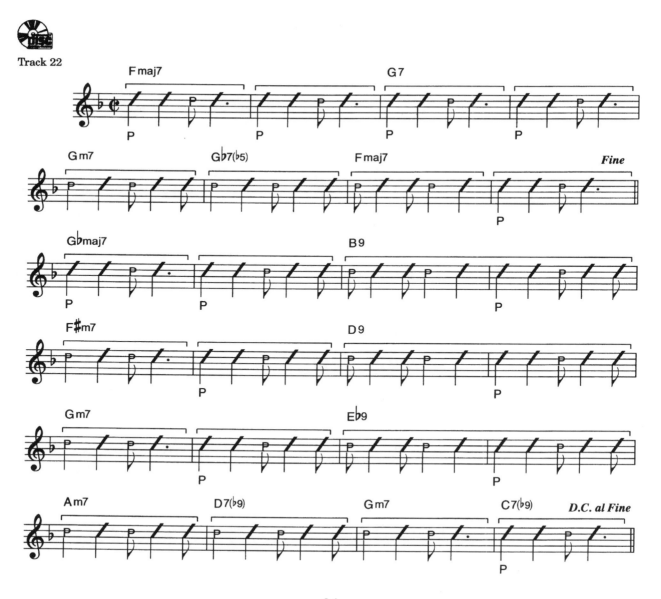

24

As mentioned earlier, although not as common as in samba, occasionally in bossa nova the bass can alternate in the measure between the root and the fifth of the chord. The next example shows how this can be done. Notice the fifth is always played below the root. If this is not possible, the root is played twice. The standard notation is written on top and the notation that has been used throughout this book is written on the bottom.

25

When two chords appear in one measure, the patterns may be divided in half, as is shown in the examples below. If the pattern being used has a finger-stroke on the "a" of beat one, change to the second chord in the measure on the "a" of beat one. The second chord in the measure anticipates the second beat. The following shows how this is done:

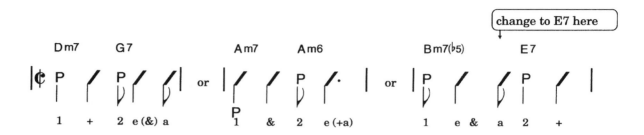

Practice the following progressions in which some measures contain two chords.

Track 24

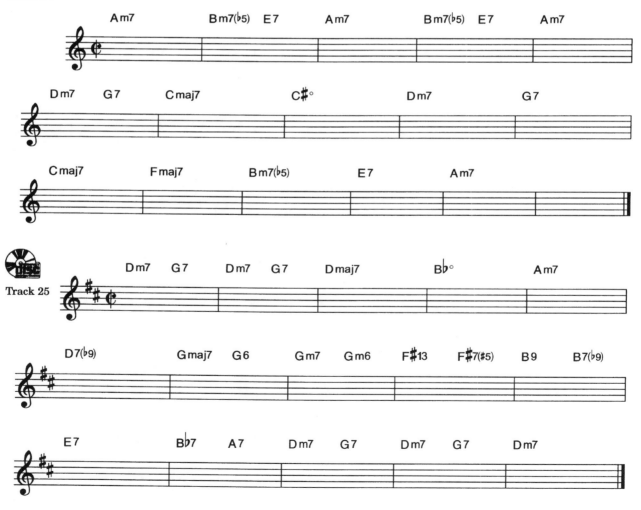

Track 25

26

SAMBA

The main difference between bossa nova style and samba lies in the accents rather than the tempo. Many of the bossa nova accompaniment patterns presented earlier can be used to play samba. In samba, there is a heavier accent on the syncopations and a more frequent used of staccato on the chord and the bass notes. The playing of the thumb on beats one and two in cut time imitates the surdo drums that are used in samba. There are three sizes of surdo drums used in samba. The very large one is played on beat two (in cut time) of every measure and is allowed to ring for the full beat. The medium-size surdo is played on beat one and is dampened. To imitate the effect of the medium and large surdo drums, whatever is played on beat two (usually thumb stroke) is a bit louder and allowed to ring. This is illustrated in the example below. Don't attempt this technique until you feel comfortable with the patterns. While this same technique can be used in bossa nova, it seems to be more characteristic of samba. The right-hand fingers are used to play the accents and are used to imitate the instrument called the *tamborim*. To make the bossa nova patterns that were presented earlier in this book sound more samba, try placing a heavier accent on beat two in each measure. Also, in samba, each of the finger strokes could be accented stronger than they would be played in bossa nova.

In bossa nova, sometimes the right-hand thumb alternates between the root of the chord and the fifth. In samba, alternating the bass between the root and the fifth is commonly done. The right-hand thumb plays the root of the chord on the first beat of the measure, and then plays the fifth of the chord (the note name which is five steps up the major scale from the root) in the middle of the measure (on beat two). The following example shows how this is done. This example is a common two-measure samba pattern. The C6/9 is played with the root on the first beat and the fifth of the chord (G) is played on beat two in cut time. In samba, the fifth of the chord should always be played below the root. If this is not possible, repeat the root. Playing the fifth below the root on beat two makes it so the right-hand thumb imitates the large surdo drum. Playing the root on beat one imitates the medium surdo drum. Notice, the first beat of the measure is short and the second beat of the measure is accented and allowed to ring. The standard notation is written on the top and the notation used in this book is written on the bottom.

Before learning the patterns in this section of the book, play the one-measure and two-measure bossa nova patterns presented on pages 20-22 into samba patterns by alternating the bass between the root and fifth (if possible) and playing the accents to get more of a samba feel.

Because in some parts of the world, sambas are considered fast, written below are some common samba accompaniment patterns that could be used at at quicker tremelo. They may also be used at a slower tempo. The first three patterns take one measure in ₵ (or $\frac{4}{4}$) to complete, and the others are two-measure patterns. The same pattern may be used through the entire piece, or several patterns may be interchanged. Practice each pattern holding one chord. Then, practice the patterns while changing random chords. As in the bossa nova patterns, if the pattern being played ends on the "a" of beat two, the new chord of the next measure will be played at that time. So, the new chord will anticipate the first beat. With many of these patterns, the thumb can be included each time the fingers are played; or, as an option, the thumb can be played with the fingers only when the P appears under the strum bar. Another possibility is to have the thumb play alone (without the fingers) where the P is written. On a more advanced level, sometimes the thumb can be totally omitted from a pattern. Pattern number 1 is the basic pattern. Most of the other patterns are variations on Pattern 1. After practicing these patterns at a slow tempo to learn them, practice them at a variety of tempos, including at a fast tempo.

Track 26

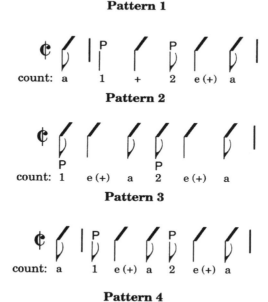

28

Pattern 5

optional before first measure   optional

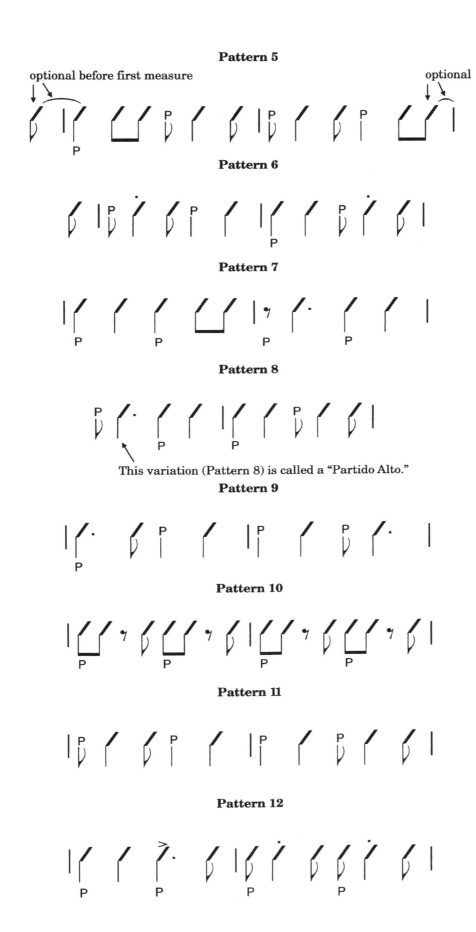

Pattern 6

Pattern 7

Pattern 8

This variation (Pattern 8) is called a "Partido Alto."

Pattern 9

Pattern 10

Pattern 11

Pattern 12

Pattern 13

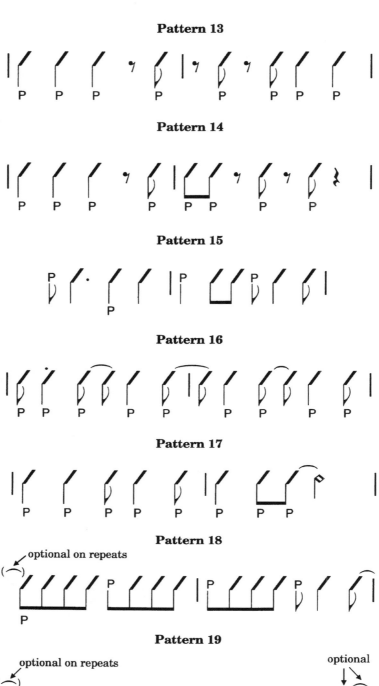

Pattern 14

Pattern 15

Pattern 16

Pattern 17

Pattern 18

optional on repeats

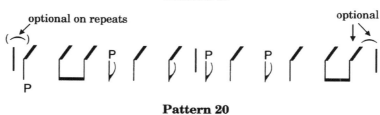

Pattern 19

optional on repeats

optional

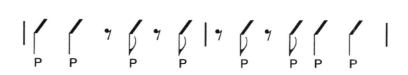

Pattern 20

30

Practice the following progressions using the samba rhythms. Once a pattern has been selected, the same pattern can be used in every measure, or more than one pattern may be used in the same piece.

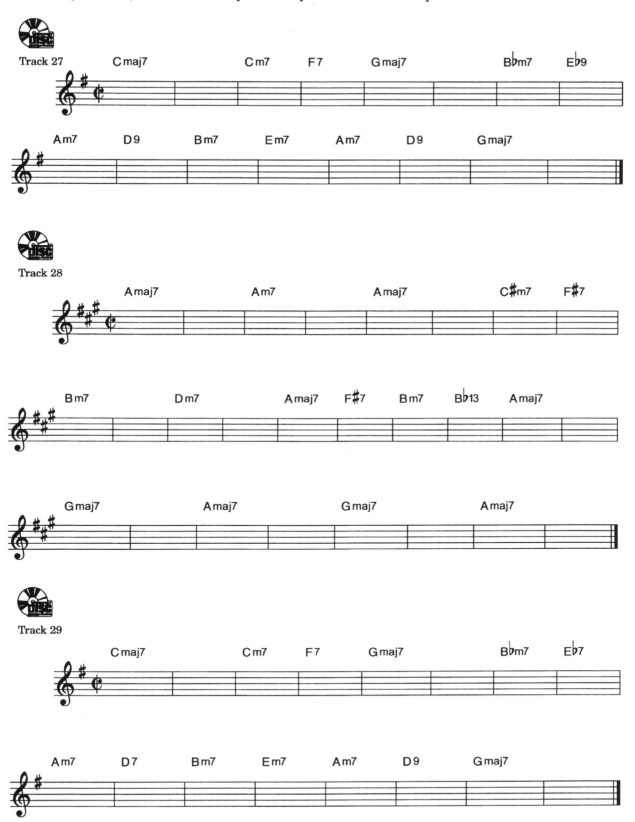

PICKSTYLE

As well as playing bossa nova and samba accompaniment with the fingers, the chords may also be strummed with a pick. Each of the patterns below takes one or two measures in ¢ to complete. The accents (>) are crucial. Be sure to place the accents in the correct place in the beat and make them subtle. Do not over-accent the accented strums. A strum bar written like this, 𝄐, is a muted strum. On these strums, lift the left-hand fingers slightly (not off of the strings) so when strummed, the strings have a muted, or dead, sound. Although it is a bit of a misconception, you may play these patterns slowly to accompany bossa novas, and quickly to accompany sambas. In playing sambas, place more emphasis on the accents and the strums that are not muted.

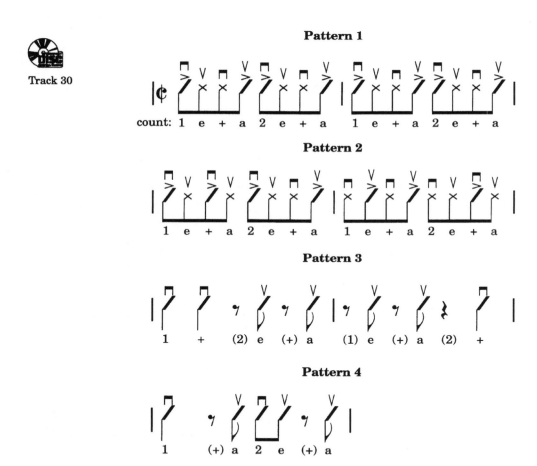

Practice the following exercises using strum patterns for ¢. The same strum pattern may be used to play each measure, or several may be interchanged.

STOP-TIME RHYTHMS

Accompaniment patterns may be interrupted with *stop-time rhythms*. Stop-time rhythms are thumb or finger-strokes followed or proceeded with rests. The right-hand thumb may be included in the strums proceeding and following the rests. The following examples show the use of stop-time rhythms.

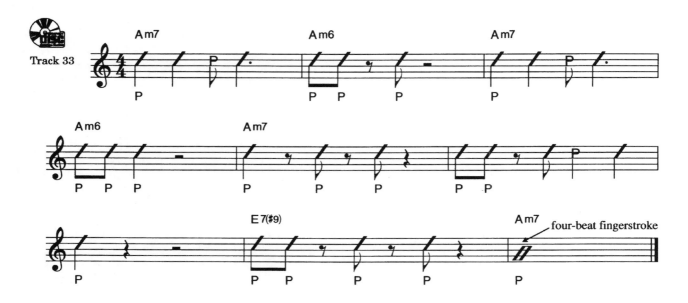

COMBINING ACCOMPANIMENT PATTERNS WITH ARPEGGIOS

The accompaniment patterns presented earlier in this book may be combined with arpeggio patterns. To accomplish this, a measure is divided in half. Half of one of the accompaniment patterns is played followed by two beats of an arpeggio. The arpeggio may be played even, but it is often syncopated. The arpeggio is often played by picking each string on the chord in succession. The arpeggios will sound best if used sparingly. The following example shows how this would be done when playing a Dm7 to a G7 to a Cmaj7.

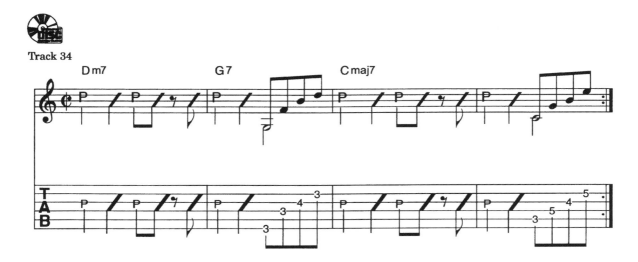

Track 34

The arpeggio may also be played on the first half of the measure followed by two beats of the accompaniment pattern. It does not matter whether the first or second half of the accompaniment pattern is used. Notice the use of syncopation in the arpeggios.

Track 35

Practice combining arpeggios with bossa nova patterns on chord progressions found earlier in this book.

COMMON CHORD PROGRESSIONS

A *chord progression* is a series of chords. Although there is not a set rule regarding the order of the chords used in a bossa nova, there are certain chord progressions that are used more frequently than others. This section of the book presents many of those progressions.

In learning common chord progressions, it is necessary to know how to identify the various keys and the chords contained in each key. To identify the key of a piece, look at the key signature. The key signature is the sharps or flats written at the beginning of each stave. If no sharps or flats are written, the music is in the key of C or A minor. If sharps are written, the name of the major key will be 1/2 step (one fret) above the last sharp sign (going left to right). If flats are written, the name of the major key will be the same as the name of the next to the last flat. One flat is the key of F or D minor. Each key signature can be major or minor. To find the minor key, first determine the major key as previously explained. Next, go one and a half steps (three frets) lower than the name of the major key. This will be the relative minor (the minor key having the same key signature). To determine if the music is in the major or minor key, look at the last chord in the piece. If it is major, the music is probably in a major key. If the last chord is minor, the music is probably in a minor key. After determining the key of the music, the chords in the key can be realized.

Each of the chords from the exercises in this section has a Roman numeral written next to it. The Roman numeral indicates which chord from the key that chord is. The I chord has the letter name of the key. The ii chord has the letter name of the second step of the major scale up from the key. The iii chord has the letter name of the third step of the major scale, and so on. Minor and half-diminished chords* are indicated with small Roman numerals, and major chords are indicated with large Roman numerals. In a major key, the I, IV, and V chords are major. The ii, iii, and vi are minor, and the vii chord is diminished.

The advantage to knowing the placement of the chord in the key is that any chord progression can be transposed into any key. For example, Dm7 to G7 to Cmaj7 is a ii-V-I progression in the key of C. If this progression were transposed to the key of F, the chords would be Gm7-C7-Fmaj7 because these are the ii-V-I chords in the key of F.

ii		V		I
Dm7	→	G7	→	Cmaj7 = key of C
Gm7	→	C7	→	Fmaj7 = key of F

* The half-diminished chord is the same as m7♭5 chord. It can be written as m7♭5 or ø.

The following chart shows the seven basic chords in each of the major keys.

CHORDS IN MAJOR KEYS

Major (key) I	Minor ii	Minor iii	Major IV	Major V	Minor VI	Diminished (if triad is used) Half-diminished (m7♭5 if embellished) vii
C	Dm	Em	F	G	Am	B$^\varnothing$
G	Am	Bm	C	D	Em	F#$^\varnothing$
D	Em	F#m	G	A	Bm	C#$^\varnothing$
A	Bm	C#m	D	E	F#m	G#$^\varnothing$
E	F#m	G#m	A	B	C#m	D#$^\varnothing$
B	C#m	D#m	E	F#	G#m	A#$^\varnothing$
F	Gm	Am	B♭	C	Dm	E$^\varnothing$
B♭	Cm	Dm	E♭	F	Gm	A$^\varnothing$
E♭	Fm	Gm	A♭	B♭	Cm	D$^\varnothing$
A♭	B♭m	Cm	D♭	E♭	Fm	G$^\varnothing$
D♭	E♭m	Fm	G♭	A♭	B♭m	C$^\varnothing$
G♭	A♭m	B♭m	C♭	D♭	E♭m	F$^\varnothing$

In a minor key, the harmonic minor scale is often used to determine the steps of the scale and the quality (major, minor, etc.). In minor, the I and iv chords are minor, the III, V, VI, and VII are major, and the ii is usually a m7♭5 (half-diminished, ø).

The following chart shows the basic chords in each of the minor keys.

CHORDS IN MINOR KEYS

Minor (key) i	Diminished (if triad is used) Half-diminished (m7♭5 if embellished) ii	Major III	Minor iv	Major V	Major VI	Major VII
Am	B$^\varnothing$	C	Dm	E	F	G
Em	F#$^\varnothing$	G	Am	B	C	D
Bm	C#$^\varnothing$	D	Em	F#	G	A
F#m	G#$^\varnothing$	A	Bm	C#	D	E
C#m	D#$^\varnothing$	E	F#m	G#	A	B
G#m	A#$^\varnothing$	B	C#m	D#	E	F#
Dm	E$^\varnothing$	F	Gm	A	B♭	C
Gm	A$^\varnothing$	B♭	Cm	D	E♭	F
Cm	D$^\varnothing$	E♭	Fm	G	A♭	B♭
Fm	G$^\varnothing$	A♭	B♭m	C	D♭	E♭
B♭m	C$^\varnothing$	D♭	E♭m	F	G♭	A♭
E♭m	F$^\varnothing$	G♭	A♭m	B♭	C♭	D♭

37

The following chart shows common chord progressions frequently appearing in bossa nova music. The first six examples are in major keys and next two are in minor keys. These progressions may be played in any key by inserting the appropriate chord corresponding to the step of the scale indicated by the Roman numeral. Practice the progressions first using the chords in parentheses (the key of C); then, play them in other keys by applying the appropriate chord for the key.

MAJOR

		IV (F)	-	V (G)	-	I (C)
		ii (Dm)	-	V (G)	-	I (C)
	vi (Am) -	ii (Dm)	-	V (G)	-	I (C)
	VI (A7) -	ii (Dm)	-	V (G)	-	I (C)
iii (Em)-	VI (A7) -	ii (Dm)	-	V (G)	-	I (C)
III (E7)-	VI (A7) -	ii (Dm)	-	V (G)	-	I (C)

MINOR

iv (Dm)	-	V (E)	-	i (Am)
ii (Bm7♭5)	-	V (E)	-	i (Am)

Practice and memorize the above progressions in all keys. These progressions will appear in many pieces.

In the following piece, notice the frequent use of the common progressions presented earlier.

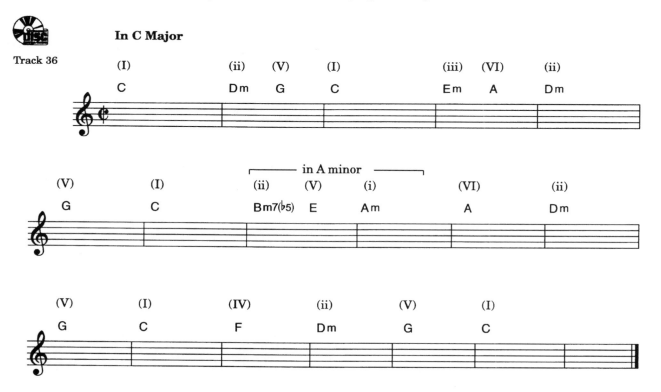

Track 36   **In C Major**

CHORD EMBELLISHMENT

One of the characteristics of the bossa nova and samba is the use of rich, sophisticated harmony. A chord is embellished when other tones are added to the basic major and minor chords creating maj7, m7, 7, 9, 13, and other chords. On the chart below, the Roman numeral on the left indicates the chord in the key, and the chord names on the right show the various types of embellishments which can be added to the chords in major and minor keys.

CHORD EMBELLISHMENTS IN MAJOR KEYS

I, IV	6, maj7, 6/9, maj9, add9, sus, maj7#11
V	sus, 7, 7sus, 9, 11, 13, 7alt (raise or lowered 5th and/or 9th)
ii, iii, vi	m6 (only on the ii chord), m7, m7sus, m+7, madd9 (minor add nine), m9
vii	diminished7 (dim), half-diminished (ø) (same as m7♭5)

CHORD EMBELLISHMENTS IN MINOR KEYS

i, iv	m6, m7, m+7, m9, madd9, m7sus
V	sus, 7, 7sus, 9, 11, 7alt (raise or lower de 5th and/or 9th)
ii	m7, m7♭5 (half-diminished ø), m+7, m7sus, m9, madd9
III, VI, VII	6, maj7, 6/9, maj9, add9, sus, maj7#11

In the following progressions, the original chords are on the bottom and the embellished chords are the top. Play the progressions un-embellished and embellished so the difference can be heard. Use bossa nova and/or samba accompaniment patterns.

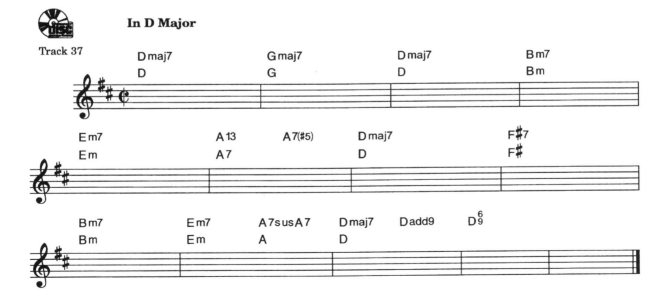

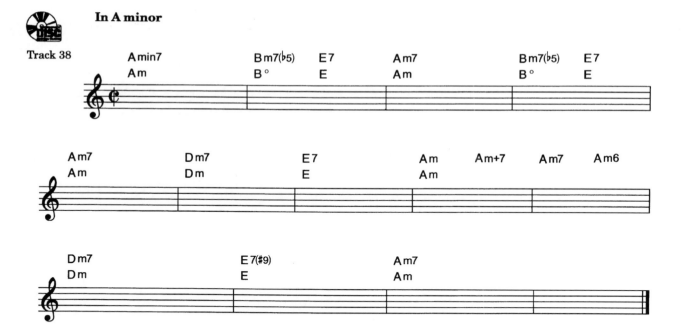

In A minor

Track 38

Amin7 / Am — Bm7(♭5) / B° — E7 / E — Am7 / Am — Bm7(♭5) / B° — E7 / E

Am7 / Am — Dm7 / Dm — E7 / E — Am / Am — Am+7 — Am7 — Am6

Dm7 / Dm — E7(♯9) / E — Am7 / Am

SLASH CHORDS

Slash chords are those in which a chord name is written followed by a slash and then a letter name (i.e. D7/C, Gmaj7/B, etc.). When a slash chord is written, play the chord on the left and place the note on the right in the bass (or as the lowest note). For example, if D7/C is written, a D7 chord is played with a C note in the bass. If the bass note cannot be placed on strings five or six, the bass note should be the lowest note in the chord. If only the top four strings are played, the added bass note should be placed on the fourth string.

F/D

Slash chords are used to connect the lowest notes of the chords. By using them, a bass line will be created to connect the chords either by half step or through a scale. The smooth- sounding chord connections achieved by using slash chords is a desired element in bossa nova and samba. In the example below, notice how Am is connected to Fmaj7 by using Am/G. This makes the chord connections smooth because G comes in between A and F in the scale.

Am   Am/G   Fmaj7

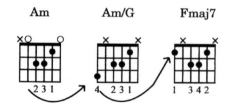

40

Common slash chords are shown below. The chords written on both sides of the slash chord show the chords which are connected by that slash chord. Practice playing one measure of the chord on the left, followed by one measure of the slash chord, then the chord on the right. Use any of the bossa nova accompaniment patterns.

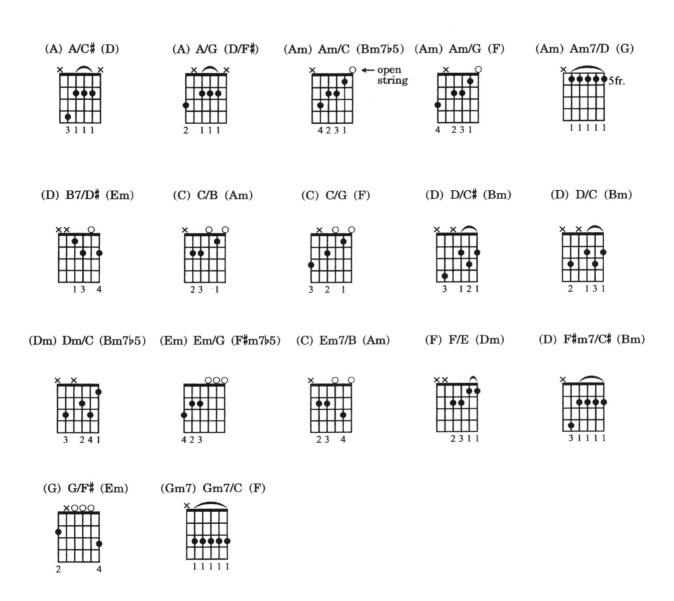

To add slash chords to an existing progression, identify the bass notes of the chords to be connected. For example, in Am7 to Fmaj7, the A note could connect to the F note. Suppose these two chords appear in a piece in the key of C. The note in the C major scale which connects A to F is G. Between the Am7 and the Fmaj7 chords, Am7/G could be played. The resulting bass line movement would be A-G-F.

Remember: when moving scalewise, the bass notes must come from the scale of the key for that section of the music.

The following progression shows how slash chords are used to create a bass line moving down and up the E minor scale.

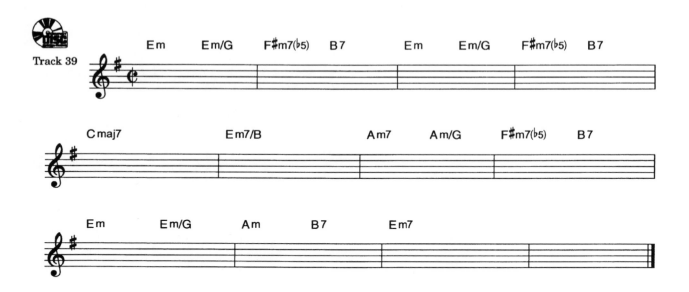

When connecting two chords which are a whole step apart, the bass line may move chromatically. For example, Dm7 to Em7 could be connected with Dm7/D#.

Play the following exercise containing slash chords.

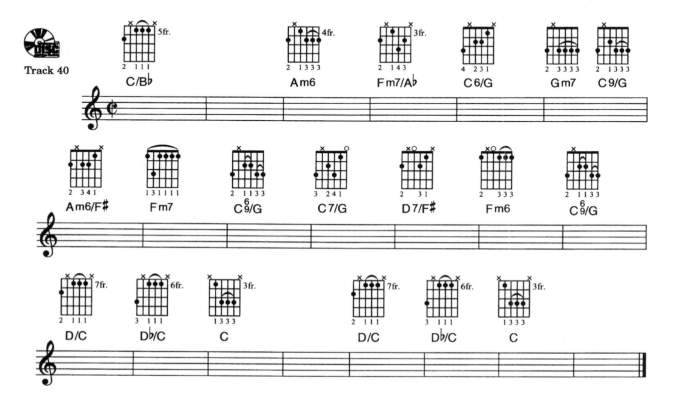

CHROMATIC BASS LINE MOVEMENT

One of the most distinguishing and beautiful characteristics of Brazilian music is the use of chromatic (half-step) bass line movement in chord changes. Very often when one chord changes to another, if all of the notes in each chord are considered, a chromatic bass line can be achieved by placing various chord tones in the bottom of the chord. For example, when playing the common chord progression, Am7-D7-Gmaj7 (ii-V-I in G), the C note (one of the notes in Am7) can be played in the bottom of the Am7 chord. The C note can be played in the bottom of the D7 chord. The C note is in the D7 chord. The B note (a chord tone of the Gmaj7 chord) can be played in the bottom of the Gmaj7 chord. The result is a short chromatic bass line movement between the D7 and Gmaj7.

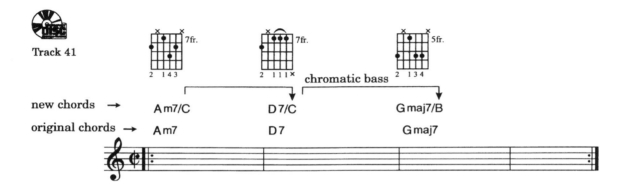

The next example shows an expanded version of the previous progression.

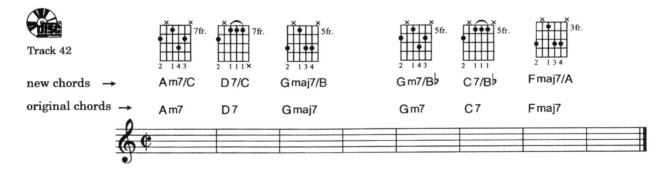

43

In the next example, a chromatic bass line has been created in the common ii-V-I progression in the key of C. Before changing the bass notes, the original chords Dm-G7-C have been embellished to become Dm9-G13-C6/9. Then, by placing the correct notes in the bottom of each chord, a chromatic bass line can be constructed. The A note is played in the bass of the Dm7 chord. An A♭ is played in the bottom of the G13 chord. This works because A♭ is the ♭9 of G13 (an embellishment of G13). The G note (a chord note of C6/9) is played in the bottom of the C6/9 chord. All of this creates a chromatic bass line to connect the chord.

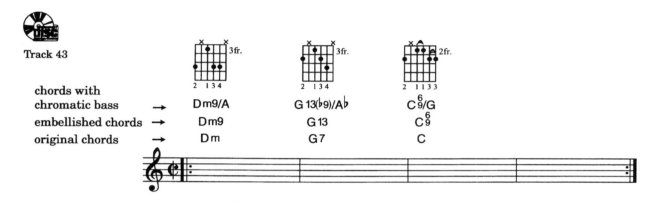

The next example shows a typical I-vi-ii-V-I chord progression in the key of C repeated several times. The chords on the bottom are the original chords, and the chords on top are substitutions and embellishments that create the chromatic bass line. Practice altering bossa novas and sambas in sheet music and lead sheets using these concepts to create interesting bass line movement.

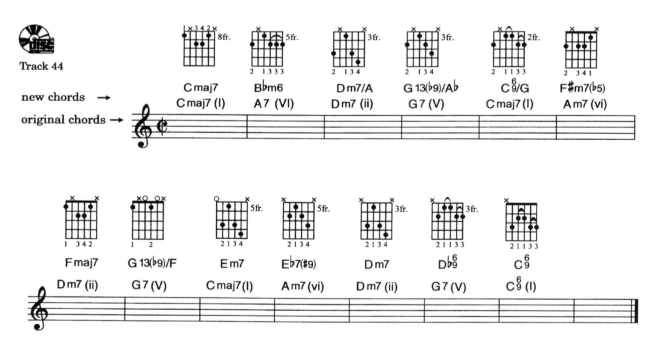

In bossa nova and samba, it is common to substitute a m6 chord that is 1/2 step higher for the V chord (ie. B♭m6 for A7). It is also common to substitute the ♭V of the V chord for the V chord (ie. E♭7 for A7).

PLAYING BOSSA NOVA AND SAMBA
SOLO GUITAR

Learning to play solo bossa nova and samba guitar could be the subject of another entire book. While there are many intricacies and techniques involved in adding the melody and playing solo guitar, the following list will provide a few basic elements for arranging bossa nova solos:

1. Always place the melody on the top of the chord. This may mean moving the melody up one octave from where it is written.

2. As much as possible, weave the melody around the bossa nova rhythm accompaniment patterns.

3. Avoid playing the melody notes on the down-beats. To achieve this, it may be good to think of cut time as 4/4. If the melody is played on the beat, move the notes rhythmically 1/2 beat earlier or 1/2 beat later so they occur on the up-beat. The example below shows how this can be done. The rhythm on the top is the original, and the rhythm on the bottom is the new version. This adjustment of the rhythm gives syncopation to the melody and helps create the Brazilian swing.

4. If the melody note is not a note in the chord, add it to the chord.

5. Small portions of the melody may be omitted. Remember, the rhythm is the important element.

6. Accent the melody notes. Bring them out.

7. At times, the accompaniment can be left out altogether and only the melody is played.

Bonita is a bossa nova guitar solo. Notice how the melody has been interwoven with the bossa nova accompaniment. The melody has been superimposed over the accompaniment pattern. Notice in measures 2, 6, and 10-13 the accompaniment (chords) are not left out, and only the single note melody is played. Also, there is strong use of syncopation and anticipation.

for Kathy

Bonita

Mike Christiansen

Coda

Made in the USA
Las Vegas, NV
22 December 2022